ROTHERHAM PUBLIC LIBRARIES

This book must be returned by the latest date entered above.
The loan may be extended [personally, by post or telephone]
for a further period if the book is not required by another reader.

LMI

Kangaroos

Christine Butterworth and Donna Bailey

MACMILLAN

The sun comes up over
the grasslands of Australia.
The animals that live here
wake up and enjoy the warm sun.

2

The kangaroo lets the warm sun
dry the morning dew on its fur.
Kangaroos feed on grass at night.
They sleep in the shade when
the day gets hot.

These are called red kangaroos.
They live together in
a crowd called a mob.

The biggest male in the mob
is called a boomer.
The boomer is as big as a tall man.
When he sits up, his tail
helps him to balance.

He also uses his tail to balance
when he fights another male.
He grabs the other kangaroo with
his front legs and kicks him
in the tummy with both back legs.

Female kangaroos are smaller
than the males.
Their fur is grey.
Can you see the baby kangaroo in
the mother's pouch?
Baby kangaroos are called joeys.

A joey lives in its mother's pouch
for nearly eight months.
The pouch is a pocket of skin on
the mother's tummy.

The mother gives the joey a wash
in the morning.
She licks the joey's fur to make it clean.
Then she licks her pouch to clean that too.

This joey is eating grass beside its mother.
It pulls up the grass with
its long front teeth.
The kangaroos are too busy to see
the wild dog creeping up on them.

Australian wild dogs are called dingoes.
Dingoes are fierce hunters.
The boomer flicks his long ears.
He can hear the dingo creeping
through the grass.

The boomer thumps his back foot
to warn the mob.
The joeys jump head first
into their mothers' pouches.

The other kangaroos in the mob run off
in all directions.
They take great hops with
their long back legs.

The joey has a fast ride
in its mother's pouch.
She jumps over a bush.
She can jump more than two metres high
off the ground.

The boomer leans back on his tail and
gets ready to kick the dingo with
his back legs.
One kick will kill the dingo.
The dingo runs off into the trees.

The other kangaroos have gone
a long way off.
When they are afraid, kangaroos
can leap more than nine metres
in one jump.
Some can travel at a speed of 30 kph.

Now the mob has come together again.
There is no more danger from the dingo so
the mob can feed and rest.
The kangaroos are tired.
They go to sleep in the shade of some trees.
This kangaroo is fast asleep on his back!

It is evening and a male kangaroo
chooses a female from the mob.
The two kangaroos will mate
during the night.

After five weeks the female
is ready to have her baby.
She leaves the mob to find
a quiet place under a tree.

The kangaroo licks her pouch clean.
She makes it ready for the new baby.
Her nipples are in her pouch.
The new baby will get milk from them.

The new-born kangaroo is tiny.
The baby looks like a little pink bean.
It is only two centimetres long.
It has no eyes or ears.

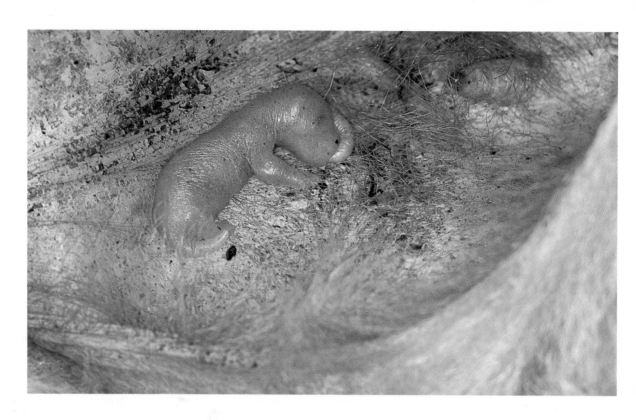

The tiny kangaroo has
little front arms and claws.
It pulls itself up the mother's fur
into her pouch.
The baby fastens its mouth onto
a nipple in the pouch.

The baby kangaroo stays inside
the mother's pouch and drinks her milk.
It grows a long tail, long ears and
long back legs.
Joeys, like the one in our picture,
do not usually climb out of the pouch.

The joey is four months old now.
It lifts its head up and
looks out of the pouch.
It is much bigger and
has grown some fur.

The joey is now big enough
to leave the pouch.
It stays near its mother and puts its head
back in her pouch to drink her milk.

A bird calls and the joey is scared.
It jumps back into her pouch.
Can you see the joey's tail as
it hides in its mother's pouch?

Now the joey is six months old.
It still drinks its mother's milk, but
it also begins to eat grass and leaves.

The joey keeps close to its mother.
She warns it if an eagle or
a fox is near by.
These animals like to eat joeys.

The mother will only let the joey
jump back into her pouch
when there is danger.
Then she carries the joey away
from the danger.

The joey is one year old.
It does not drink the mother's milk
any more.
She has another tiny kangaroo
in her pouch now.

The joey joins the rest of the mob.
The kangaroos keep a sharp look out
for any enemies.

Some joeys in the mob
are nearly two years old.
They are ready to go off and
live by themselves.

Reading consultant: Diana Bentley
Editorial consultant: Donna Bailey

Illustrated by Paula Chasty
Picture research by Suzanne Williams
Designed by Richard Garratt Design

This edition specially produced for
Macmillan Children's Books,
a division of Macmillan Publishers Limited

First published 1989

This edition published by
Macmillan Children's Books,
a division of Macmillan Publishers Limited
4 Little Essex Street, London WC2R 3LF and Basingstoke
Associated companies around the world.

Printed in Hong Kong

British Library Cataloguing in Publication Data
Butterworth, Christine
   Kangaroos.
   1.   English Language. Readers - For children
   I.   Title   II. Bailey, Donna III. Series
   428.6
   ISBN 0-333-48668-4

Photographs
Cover: Frank Lane Picture Agency/W Wisniewski
Bruce Coleman: titlepage, 5, 12, 13, 14, 16, 18, 20 and 31 (Jen &
   Des Bartlett), 8 (Jan Taylor), 17 (Hans Reinhard), 21 (Alan
   Root), 22 (Vincent Serventy), 23 (Graham Pizzey), 26 (J
   Cancalosi), 32 (John Wallis)
Frank Lane Picture Agency: 6 and 15 (W Wisniewski), 24 and 25
   (Carlo Dani Ingrid Jeske c Silvestris)
NHPA: 2 (ANT), 7, 9, 27 and 30 (Patrick Fagot), 19 (Ken
   Griffiths)